SandCastle

Word Families Set 5

-ot as in knot

Amanda Rondeau

Consulting Editor Monica Marx, M.A./Reading Specialist

ABDO
Publishing Company

Published by SandCastle™, an imprint of ABDO Publishing Company, 4940 Viking Drive, Edina, Minnesota 55435.

Printed in the United States.

Credits
Edited by: Pam Price
Curriculum Coordinator: Nancy Tuminelly
Cover and Interior Design and Production: Mighty Media
Photo Credits: BananaStock Ltd., Corbis, Hemera, PhotoDisc, Stockbyte

Library of Congress Cataloging-in-Publication Data

Rondeau, Amanda, 1974-
    -Ot as in knot / Amanda Rondeau.
       p. cm. -- (Word families. Set V)
    Summary: Introduces, in brief text and illustrations, the use of the letter combination "ot" in such words as "knot," "dot," "plot," and "forgot."
    ISBN 1-59197-253-1
    1. Readers (Primary) [1. Vocabulary. 2. Reading.] I. Title.

PE1119 .R698 2003
428.1--dc21   2002038214

SandCastle™ books are created by a professional team of educators, reading specialists, and content developers around five essential components that include phonemic awareness, phonics, vocabulary, text comprehension, and fluency. All books are written, reviewed, and leveled for guided reading, early intervention reading, and Accelerated Reader® programs and designed for use in shared, guided, and independent reading and writing activities to support a balanced approach to literacy instruction.

Let Us Know

After reading the book, SandCastle would like you to tell us your stories about reading. What is your favorite page? Was there something hard that you needed help with? Share the ups and downs of learning to read. We want to hear from you! To get posted on the ABDO Publishing Company Web site, send us e-mail at:

sandcastle@abdopub.com

SandCastle Level: Transitional

-ot Words

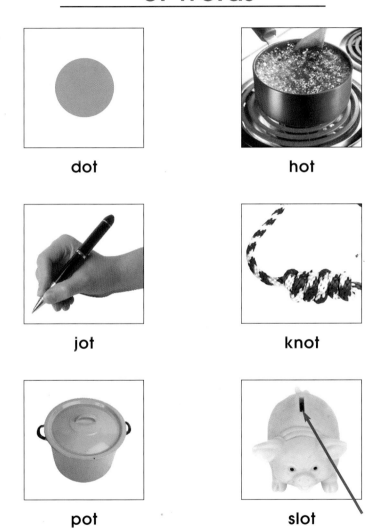

dot

hot

jot

knot

pot

slot

Jen has more than one
dot on her shirt.

Kyle likes to swim on a hot day.

Alex can jot a note on a card for her dad.

Uncle Tim shows us how to tie a knot.

Dale helps stir the
sauce in a big pot.

Mom put a coin in the slot.

Scot the Hotshot

Scot thought
he was a real hotshot.

He could tie
the biggest knot.

In basketball
he made every shot.

He could do everything
his brothers could not.

So he thought he should
have the biggest cot.

At home he always
got the best spot.

He was the center
of every snapshot.

But soon Scot's brothers wanted a shot

at the biggest cot

and the best spot.

"You're right," said Scot.
"I almost forgot!"

"Sharing is better than being a hotshot."

The -ot Word Family

cot	not
dot	plot
forgot	pot
got	Scot
hot	shot
hotshot	slot
jot	snapshot
knot	spot

Glossary

Some of the words in this list may have more than one meaning. The meaning listed here reflects the way the word is used in the book.

basketball   a game where the players bounce a ball and try to throw it through a high hoop

brother   a male who has the same parents as another person

share   to divide something between people or take turns using something

snapshot   a photograph

swim   to move through the water by moving your arms and legs

About SandCastle™

A professional team of educators, reading specialists, and content developers created the SandCastle™ series to support young readers as they develop reading skills and strategies and increase their general knowledge. The SandCastle™ series has four levels that correspond to early literacy development in young children. The levels are provided to help teachers and parents select the appropriate books for young readers.

Emerging Readers
(no flags)

Beginning Readers
(1 flag)

Transitional Readers
(2 flags)

Fluent Readers
(3 flags)

These levels are meant only as a guide. All levels are subject to change.

To see a complete list of SandCastle™ books and other nonfiction titles from ABDO Publishing Company, visit **www.abdopub.com** or contact us at:

4940 Viking Drive, Edina, Minnesota 55435 • 1-800-800-1312 • fax: 1-952-831-1632